ALSO BY ROBERT CREELEY

Le Fou (1952)
The Kind Of Act Of (1953)
The Immoral Proposition (1953)
The Gold Diggers (1954, 1965)
All That Is Lovely in Men (1955)
A Form of Women (1959)
For Love: Poems 1950-1960 (1962)
The Island (1963)
Words (1965, 1967)
Poems 1950-1965 (1966)
The Finger (with Bobbie Creeley) (1968)
The Charm (1968, 1969)
Numbers (1968)
Pieces (with Bobbie Creeley) (1968, 1969)
The Finger: Poems 1966-1969 (1970)
A Quick Graph (1970)
St. Martin's (with Bobbie Creeley) (1971)
1-2-3-4-5-6-7-8-9-0 (with Arthur Okamura) (1971)
Listen (with Bobbie Creeley) (1972)
A Day Book (1972)
Contexts of Poetry: Interviews 1961-1971 (1973)
Thirty Things (with Bobbie Creeley) (1974)
Presences (with Marisol) (1976)

ROBERT CREELEY

AWAY

ILLUSTRATIONS BY

BOBBIE CREELEY

BLACK SPARROW PRESS

SANTA BARBARA · 1976

LIBRARY OF CONGRESS CATALOGING IN PUBLICATION DATA

Creeley, Robert, 1926-
  Away.

  I. Title.
PS3505.R43A94   811'.5'4   76-41400
ISBN 0-87685-278-9 (paper edition)
ISBN 0-87685-279-7 (trade cloth edition)
ISBN 0-87685-280-0 (signed cloth edition)

One can own a mirror; does one then own the reflection that can be seen in it?

Wittgenstein, *Zettel*

Table of Contents

AWAY

AWAY

for Bobbie

Yourself walked in the room tonight
and it wasn't you. Your way of
being here isn't another's way.
It's all the same somewhere maybe,
and the same old thing isn't you.
All the negatives in existence
don't change anything anyway.

.

The people tell me a sad story sometimes,
and I tend to tell it back to them.

.

Come home. It's where you are anyway.
Anyway I wish you weren't home.
Where is home anyway without me.

.

This place could be rolled up
and put away. Somebody
could warn the so-called people.

11

I wish I could talk to the people
without going away. Home,
wherever, is where the heart is.

I don't want to talk to the people,
where the heart is. It's home
you and me talk for hours.

.

For hours I didn't think of you
and then I did and can't stop.

.

Your birthday is here
without you, that day
you were born to be here.

The loveliest day I saw you
buying your first car
with such a lovely presence, of mind.

It doesn't work without you.
I do, it doesn't. Funny
or not, it's no good.

I'll be home, all ways—
you name it. I'll put a ribbon
on it. You're my love.

.

Cross in my mind, wanting,
waiting, to get home again.
A kind of weird road
stuck in the middle.

Whatever else it is,
love is the middle
with you and me
right in the middle.

The middle of midnight
is what time it is,
two hours earlier than you,
and me going nowhere.

Only the same time,
your birthday. You and me
at the same time in
the same place, always.

EVERY DAY

Every day
in a little way
things are done.

Every morning there is
a day. Every day
there is a day.

Waking up in a bed
with a window with light,
with a place in mind,

to piss, to eat,
to think of something,
to forget it all,

to remember everything,
perfectly, each
specific, actual detail,

knowing nothing,
having no sense of any of it,
not being a part of it,

all right for you,
all right, you guys—
echoes, things, faces.

SOUND

Hearing a car pass—
that insistent distance
from here to there,
sitting here.

Sunlight
shines through the green leaves,
patterns of light and dark,
shimmering.

But so quiet
now the car's gone,
sounds of myself smoking,
my hand writing.

HERE

No one
else in the room
except you.

.

Mind's a form
of taking
it all.

.

And the room
opens
and closes.

1971

The year the head
went out into a
field and hid
there. The year
the water came
higher than the edges—

all the people,
all the ways of
getting here and
now, here and
now here.

BERLIN: FIRST NIGHT
& EARLY MORNING

I've lost place,
coming here.
The space's noises,

trucks outside, cars
shifting, voices I
can't understand the

words of—how
long ago all this
was otherwise? Tired,

time lost, the room's
narrow size, patience
to be here useless.

All done
long ago, all
gone now.

        .

Cough's explicit
continuity. Little
birds twitter.

        .

The key has a
big metal thing attached
to it, flattened, then

becoming a ball
at one end, with
a rubber washer around it.

.

Six thirty now.
Air France.

.

Tame. Marlboro.
Comb and ticket.

.

Not me only
without you—

.

Oh so nice
to be awake
after no sleep
all night.

.

Last night, walking,
the street was slabs
of wild color, signs,
so much to bring to mind.

Things to sell, a long
horizontal of store fronts,

cars, radios, books, and food.
Clothes—people walking too.

.

Absence makes
the heart break
a little bit
wanting out.

.

You: "too abstract,
try it,
all,
over again . . ."

.

Money's got
stylized eagle
on it and a cold
looking man with bald head.

I had to put
on my glasses to
make out its value
while they waited.

They live here,
these people.
Kontakt Linsen,
Abel Optik.

Let us *tanzen*
miteinander
and make love
to *dem Mond.*

FOR MY MOTHER:
GENEVIEVE JULES CREELEY
April 8, 1887—October 7, 1972

Tender, semi-
articulate flickers
of your

presence, all
those years
past

now, eighty-
five, impossible to
count them

one by one, like
addition, sub-
traction, missing

not one. The last
curled up, in
on yourself,

position you take
in the bed, hair
wisped up

on your head, a
top knot, body
skeletal, eyes

closed against,
it must be,
further disturbance—

breathing a skim
of time, lightly
kicks the intervals—

days, days and
years of it,
work, changes,

sweet flesh caught
at the edges,
dignity's faded

dilemma. It
is *your* life, oh
no one's

forgotten anything
ever. They want
to make you

happy when
they remember. Walk
a little, get

up, now, die
safely,
easily, into

singleness, too
tired with it
to keep

on and on.
Waves break at
the darkness

under the road, sounds
in the faint
night's softness. Look

at them, catching
the light, white
edge as they turn—

always again
and again. Dead
one, two,

three hours—
all these minutes
pass. Is it,

was it, ever
you alone
again, how

long you kept
at it, your
pride, your

lovely, confusing
discretion. Mother, I
love you—for

whatever that
means,
meant—more

than I know, body
gave me my
own, generous,

inexorable place
of you. I feel
the mouth's sluggish-

ness, slips on
turns of things
said, to you,

too soon, too late,
wants to
go back to beginning,

smells of the hospital
room, the doctor
she responds

to now, the
order—get me
there. "Death's

let you out—"
comes true,
this, that,

endlessly circular
life, and we
came back

to see you one
last
time, this

time? Your head
shuddered,
it seemed, your

eyes wanted,
I thought,
to see

who it was.
I am here,
and will follow.

FUNNY

Raining here
in little pieces
of rain.
Wet, brother,

behind the ears,
I love your hands.
And you too,
rain.

You insist on rain
because you are
no less than water,
no more than wet.

OUT

Let me walk to you
backwards
down a long street.

.

Here is the rain again.
I hear it
in my ear here.

.

What fun
to be done
if not already
done.

.

We were going
out.

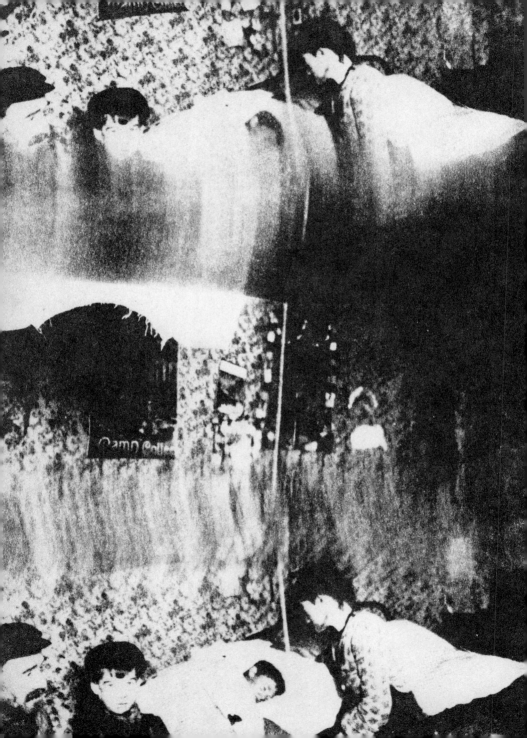

HERE AGAIN

After we
were all
a bed,
a door, two
windows
and a chair.

THE PLAN IS THE BODY

The plan is the body.
There is each moment a pattern.
There is each time something
for everyone.

The plan is the body.
The mind is in the head.
It's a moment in time,
an instant, second.

The rhythm of one
and one, and one, and one.
The two, the three.
The plan is *in* the body.

Hold it an instant,
in the mind—hold it.
What was said you
said. The two, the three,

times in the body,
hands, feet, you remember—
I, I remember, I
speak it, speak it.

The plan is the body.
Times you didn't want to,
times you can't think
you want to, *you.*

Me, *me,* remember, me
here, me wants to, *me*
am thinking of *you.*
The plan is the body.

The plan is the body.
The sky is the sky.
The mother, the father—
the plan is the body.

Who can read it.
Plan is the body. The mind
is the plan. *I*—
speaking. The memory

gathers like memory, plan,
I thought to remember,
thinking again, thinking.
The mind is the plan of the mind.

The plan is the body.
The plan is the body.
The plan is the body.
The plan is the body.

BLUE

Ice not
wet not
hot not
white.

Ice cold.

DEAR DOROTHY

for Dorothy Dean

Dear Dorothy,
I thought a lot
of what you said—
the gentle art of being nice—

For finks—for you,
"just let me out—
fuck off, you creeps!"
I'd like to get it right

for once, not spend all
fucking life in patience.
I get scared of getting
lost, I hold on hard

to you. Your voice was
instantly familiar. My middle
agéd hippy number
is more words, I like

the tone and place.
I like to drink
and talk to people,
all the lovely faces.

But in the car I'm driving
back to some place on
West Broadway, a man is making
faces at me through the window—

scared, confused at why he
wants to do that. *Why* the
constant pain. It always
hurts—hence drive away

from him. Or, drinking,
go into the men's room,
then come out to
indescribable horrors, lights,

and people *eating* people,
awful. Sounds and noises,
horror, scream at
"what's the matter?" *don't*

you *ever* touch me—
wanting love so much.
Can shake for hours with
thinking, scared it's all got lost . . .

"Would you *fuck* that?"
"My God!" Your ineluctable
smile, it falls back in your head,
you *smile* with such a gentle

giving up. I sadly loved
it that you wopped me with your purse.
"Stupid!" I think of things,
I'm loyal. Narcissist, I want.

THAN I

I'm telling you a
story to let myself
think about it. All

day I've been
here, and yesterday.
The months, years,

enclose me as
this thing with arms
and legs. And if

it *is* time
to talk about it,
who knows better

than I?

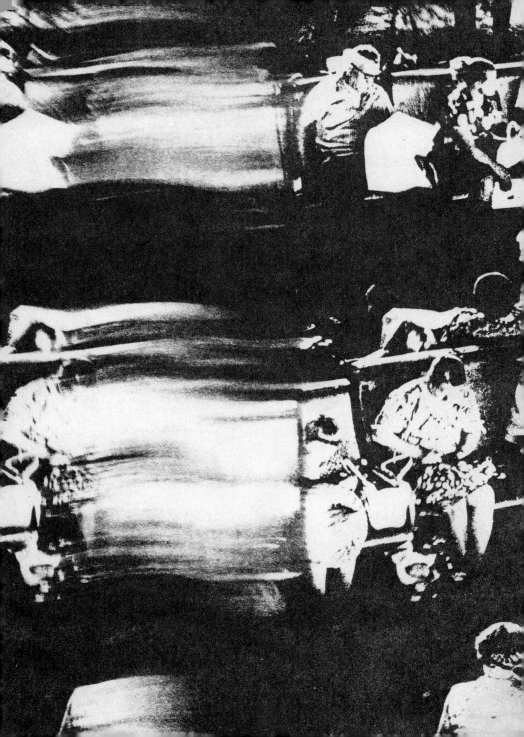

COMFORT

Staggering, you know
they fall
forward to

their desire. Garbage,
pain, people,

want it all,
their comfort
every time.

DREAMS

Tunneling through the earth
this way, I didn't know

the surface was where
I had come from. Dreams.

SHOT

The bubble breaking
of reflecting mirrors.
Water.

FALLING

Falling
from grace—
umpteenth time
rain's hit my head,
generous water.

SLEEP

Matrix of your legs,
charming woman,
handholds of firm

proportion—flesh figures in
the signs. Days away
from said past,

backwards "is no
direction?" Thought once,
twice—woke in night

several times as the furniture,
in the dream, backed out
the door, carried by affable

frightening people. Son-
in-law was depressed,
sitting on bed, daughter

beside him—how
had I misunderstood? Me
saying, "no, I

didn't"—little murmur
of self-content? Am
fearful, following

the couch, they have it,
into room occupied by
gang. Hence wake up

without you, bed warm,
sky grey, the day now
to come.

CIRCLE

As from afar,
through ringlet of woods,
the huntsman stares in wonder

at the sight, delight
in that light haze of circle
seems to surround you.

.

Crashing sound, the woods
move. Leaves fluttering,
birds making chatter—
your body sans error.

.

Pounds the musculature
where flesh joins bone—
hangs loose, thus
relieves.

.

Several melding persons,
one face, one
mirror in which to see it?

.

Expanse of trees
going up block
the light coming down
to us sitting here.

.

Rolls in laughter,
black hair, generous
action of your body.

.

Woods all over the place,
find them forever
apparently
where you are.

.

Isolated,
to think
of you, of you—

sea's plunging forms
and sounds, rock
face, the white, recurring

edge of foam—
love's forms
are various.

.

In the circle of this
various woods,
one presence, persistent,

shines. An easy seeming
extension of her light
continually brings me to her.

.

EASE

A day's
pattern
broken,
by your love.

.

Come here
(come home)
to think

of you
(of you).

.

A bird
for you, a singing
bird.

.

I'd climb into
your body
if I could, cover

myself up entirely
in your generous
darkening body,

steal away all
senses, sleep
in the hole.

.

You, you, you—
one and only.

.

What use love—
to make me cry,
to make me laugh?

.

Flood of details, memory's
delight—the sight
of you.

.

Waves rolling over,
continuously, sound
of much being done.

Get up, for actions—
impedes the sight, hearing,
—want to walk away?

Stay here. Where I am,
is alone here, on the sand.
Water out in front of me

crashes on.

.

KID

"What are you doing?"
Writing some stuff.

"You a poet?"
Now and then.

.

Woods, water,
all you
are.

.

And the particular
warmth of you,
all asleep
together.

.

WATER

As much to know you,
love, to witness this changing surface
from so constant a place.

.

I'll never get it right enough,
will never stop trying.

.

Old one-eye,
fish head,
wants his water back.

Dear friend,
bring bucket
and shovel.

.

Truly see you,
surfacing, all

slippery, wetness,
at home.

.

If I wanted
to know myself,
I'd look at you.

When I loved
what I was,
it was that reflection.

.

Color so changing here,
sky lightens, water

greens, blues.
Never far from you,

no true elsewhere.
My hands stay with me.

.

You'd think the years
would change some first sense

of whatever it is—
but it comes again and again.

.

Love's watery condition
waits only for you.

*Perfection of substance
leaps high in lacy foam.*

Deep as it goes,
entirely you.

Wind gets chill,
sun trying to shine.
Move on again.

In the world a few
things to think of,
a blessing.

I don't love
to prove it—love
to know it.

Bixby Canyon, July 10, 1973

FOR A BUS ON ITS SIDE
AND THE MAN INSIDE IT

Wise house, and
man to know it,

thinks with nothing
farther than arm's reach,

the room of space,
the place of body's

home, ground, grass,
trees, sky, water's

distance, books, all
one in this clear place.

FOR WALTER CHAPPELL

Dream: pigeon—
rooftop, water,
car window

open, crashes in,
get it back there.
The race, against time?

What matter.
Wander with
skin and hands

on my back, my
head, my eye,
tired of ways to get by.

Flying by, flying
off, the roof,
whirls of air,

light sequences, that
setting sun, rock,
stubbed toe against,

I held to, sunk
under it, way
down, such roots

as rocks and trees,
the wind, seem
wise to.

Loving days, loving
eyes, loving
you, loving

ways of loving.
*What's here is
elsewhere, nothing's*

not—don't worry, I
see. See it all
now, open

head surf crashes
through. And
lovely light attentive,

dripping fissures,
all the world,
the world.

If in or out
of it, your friendship
saw the eye

we swam in, brother—
deep ditch with children,
warm nights with water,

sweetening, silver light
become the place
we came to.

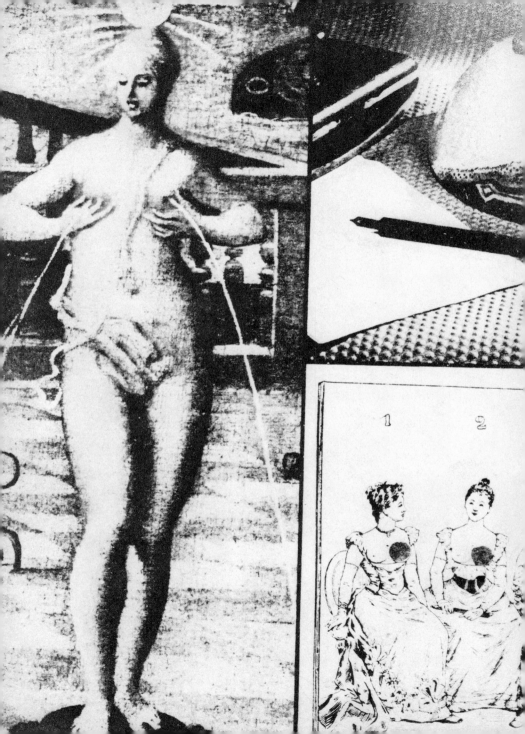

"THERE . . ."

There is a world
underneath, or
on top of,
this one—and
it's here, now.

EASTER

Don't
ever refuse
the

people
in their
place.

PHONE

What the words,
abstracted, tell:
specific agony,

pain of one so
close, so distant—
abstract here—

Call back, call
to her—smiling voice.
Say, it's all right.

SICK

**Belly's full
of rubble.**

SITTING HERE

Roof's peak is eye,
sky's grey, tree's
a stack of lines,

wires across it. This
is window, this is
sitting at the table,

thinking of you,
far away,
whose face is

by the mirror on the bureau.
I love you, I said,
because I wanted to,

because I know you,
my daughter, my
daughter.

I don't want you
to walk away. I
get scared

in this loneliness.
Be *me* again
being born, be the little

wise one walks
quietly by, in the sun,
smiles silently,

grows taller and taller.
Because all these things
passing, changing,

all the things
coming and going
inside, outside—

I can't hold them,
I want to but
keep on losing them.

As if to catch your hand, then,
your fingers, to hang on,
as if to feel

it's all right here
and will be, that
world *is* wonder,

being simply beyond us,
patience its savor,
and to keep moving,

we love what we love,
what we have,
what we have to.

I don't know—
this fact of time spinning,
days, weeks, months, years,

stuffed in some attic.
Or—where can we run,
why do I want to?

As if that touch of you
had, unknowing,
turned me around again

truly to face you,
and your face is wet,
blurred, with tears—

or is it simply years later,
sitting here, and whatever
we were has gone.

UP IN THE AIR

Trees
breathing
air.

.

No longer
closely here
no longer.

.

Fire still burning
in heart. People
move in the oak brush.
Day widens,
music in the room.
Think it's back
where you left it?
Think, think
of nothing.

.

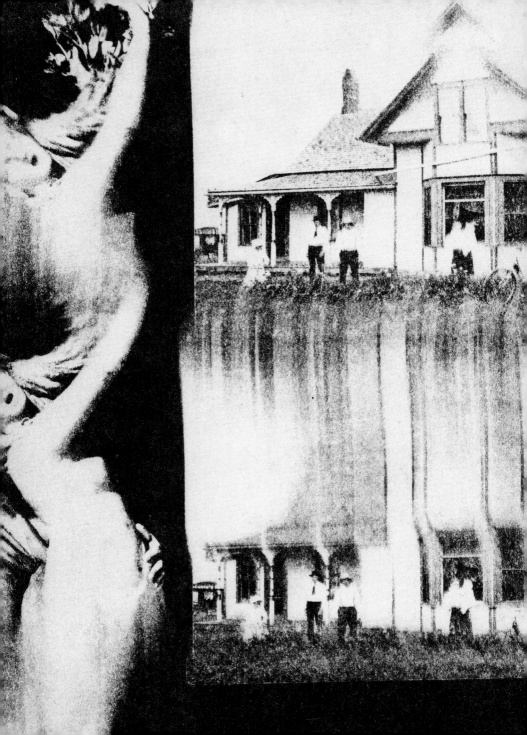

Mind tremors,
(taught) taut rubber,
shimmers of bounce.

·

Sensual body,
a taut skin?

Not the same
mistake "twice"?

Reechoes, re-
collects.

·

Each one
its own imagination

"at best"

·

This
can be thought of?

of

·

Tree tops
your head

·

"That's very frequent in French."

·

Indignity
no name

.

Those old hotels.

.

"I'm going to take a trip
in that old gospel ship

"I'm going far beyond the sky

—"bid this world goodbye"

"I can scarcely wait . . .
I'll spend my time in prayer—"

"And go sailing through
          the air . . ."

If you are ashamed of me,
you ought not to be . . .

You will sure be left behind,
while *I'm* sailing through

          the air . . .

.

Beauty's desire shall be endless
and a hell of a lot of fun.

.

Luck?
Looks like.

.

Falls
always.

.

You go
that way.
I'll
go this.

.

Many times broke
but never poor.
Many times poor
but never broke.

.

Be welcome
to it.

.

Mind-
ful of feeling,

thinking it.

.

Sun's hand's shadow.
Air passes. Friends.

.

The right one.
The wrong one.
The other one.

.

Heavy time moves
imponderably present.

.

Let her
sing it
for herself.

.

Keep a distance
recovers space.

San Cristobal, N.M.
May 29, 1974

Printed September 1976 in Santa Barbara & Ann Arbor
for the Black Sparrow Press by Mackintosh & Young
and Edwards Brothers Inc. Design by Barbara Martin.
This edition is published in paper wrappers; there are
500 cloth trade copies; an additional 200 hardcover
copies have been numbered & signed by the author;
& 50 numbered copies containing an original color print
by Bobbie Creeley have been handbound in boards by
Earle Gray & are signed by the author & artist.

ROBERT CREELEY was born in Arlington, Mass., in 1926. After a period at Harvard, he left without completing a degree to drive an ambulance for the American Field Service in India and Burma. He has lived also in Guatemala, France, and Mallorca, where he ran the Divers Press. He received a B.A. from Black Mountain College and taught there from 1954 to 1956, also editing the *Black Mountain Review.* He has since taught at the University of New Mexico, the University of British Columbia, San Francisco State College, and currently at the State University of New York at Buffalo. He has previously published five books with Black Sparrow Press, *The Finger* (1968), *Pieces* (1968), *St. Martin's* (1971), *Listen* (1972) and *Thirty Things* (1974).

BOBBIE CREELEY is both an artist and a writer. In addition to illustrating the five Black Sparrow books listed above, she illustrated *air the trees* by Larry Eigner (1968) and *Blake's Newton* by Michael Palmer (1972). As a writer, she has published both poetry and prose, using the name Bobbie Louise Hawkins. *Own Your Body*, a group of poems, was published by Black Sparrow in 1973, and Ms. Hawkins has two prose books scheduled for Fall 1976 publication, *Back to Texas* and *Stories*.